*Level Green*

# The Brittingham Prize in Poetry

The University of Wisconsin Press Poetry Series
Ronald Wallace, GENERAL EDITOR

*Places/Everyone*
Jim Daniels

*Talking to Strangers*
Patricia Dobler

*Saving the Young Men of Vienna*
David Kirby

*Pocket Sundial*
Lisa Zeidner

*Slow Joy*
Stefanie Marlis

*Level Green*
Judith Vollmer

Judith Vollmer

---

*Level Green*

The University of Wisconsin Press

The University of Wisconsin Press
114 North Murray Street
Madison, Wisconsin 53715

3 Henrietta Street
London WC2E 8LU, England

5   4   3   2

Printed in the United States of America


Library of Congress Cataloging-in-Publication Data
Vollmer, Judith, 1951–
    Level green / Judith Vollmer.
        96 pp.        cm. — (The Brittingham prize in poetry)
    I. Title.   II. Series.
    PS3572.03957L48        1990
    811'.54 — dc20        90-50101
    ISBN 0-299-12750-8
    ISBN 0-299-12754-0 (pbk.)

This book is for Violette Leduc
*In Memoriam*

# Contents

## III

# Acknowledgments

Acknowledgments are due the editors of the following magazines and anthologies for first or forthcoming publication of many of these poems:

*Hanging Loose*: "Nursing the Sunburn"
*Laurel Review*: "Fabian," "The Man in the Gray House"
*the minnesota review*: "My Grandmother's Rags"
*One Shot*: "To the Female Rockstars, 1985"
*Prairie Schooner*: "Smoking Cigars with Li Po," "To Hera"
*Southern Poetry Review*: "Motel, on the Anniversary of the Death of John Belushi"
*Synthesis*: "Wildsisters Bar"
*Tar River Poetry*: "Troy Hill Voices"
*West Branch*: "Sara's Terrace," "The Bracelet"
*The Women's Review of Books*: "Father's Magic Trick," "The Nuclear Accident at SL 1, Idaho Falls, 1961"
"Fourteen Nights" appeared in *Living Inland*, an anthology of women poets and photographers of Western Pennsylvania, Bennington Press, Pittsburgh, eds. Judith Robinson and Patricia Dobler, 1989.
"Sara's Terrace" was included in the 1987 *Anthology of Magazine Verse*.
"Music Lessons" is forthcoming in the anthology *Preposterous: Poems of Youth*, Orchard Books, New York, ed. Paul B. Janeczko, 1991.
"Nursing the Sunburn," "To the Female Rockstars, 1985," and "Wildsisters Bar" are forthcoming in *Sweet Nothings: An Anthology of Rock and Roll in American Poetry*, Spoon River Press, Peoria, ed. Jim Elledge, 1991.
Line 27 of "Thaw" is from Neil Young's song, "Rapid Transit," from the *Reactor* album.
Quotes in "Palomas Fountain" are from Eva Forest's book, *From a Spanish Prison*.

Thanks to the Pennsylvania Council on the Arts for a poetry fellowship which aided in the completion of several of the poems; to Ann Stokes, for a residency at Welcome Hill; to the women of Wildsisters Coffeehouse, to my parents, Regis and Marie Vollmer, and to the many poets and friends in Western Pennsylvania who have helped me with individual poems in this book.

Finally, heartfelt thanks to Ann Begler, Patricia Dobler, Lynn Emanuel and Ed Ochester for their longstanding editorial guidance and personal support.

*Level Green*

# *Thaw*

*Death to identity*! Life says to us:
each of us is the other, goodbye
to one body in order to enter another!
—Neruda

Last night, lonely, I couldn't sleep.
Today I'm full of sky.
I'm Anna Pavlova biting grapes in "Bacchanale,"
torn ribbon tied around my head. Gray mist
and no coat. New clogs. Hair washed and getting damp
all over again.
Semiprecious stones hold my bed up
and I'm looking for new ones
on Agate Way. I take my stroll,
turn out all the rocks in my head
and every one loves the light.
I'm so transparent I'm a drop of quartz,
I'm jade, I'm the laughing boy straddling the boar's back
or the stately cricket, wings folded in intricate solitude
or the Egyptian cat whose intelligent head is yet another reminder
of what we can choose and follow
if we stay supple enough.
My brain is filled with pearls.
I need them to get my heavy reading done.
I'm reading Propertius
who didn't worry about self-indulgence
as much as I think I have to.
He put his jealous heart on ice while he worked:
he sat, wrote, something gave back grand permission.
I yield to the mineral kingdom.
I yield to the New Age, though
every wave is new until it breaks.
I yield to the *David* & the *Venus*
and they sit down beside me.

If words are flesh
stone is water and my love is like
a whitewater ride in early June.
I dig my knees & heels into the pliant boat, stay very still
while the river fans its
huge wall over & onto us.
I sleep beside lovers
whose teeth glisten with my juices.
We don't want to live forever
just long enough.
If stone is water
my heart's floating off
with all my treasures:
her hard work, his eyes,
his wild talk, her hair.
Birds from my old life offer directions home.
I go when I can, back over cobbled streets
rinsed bronze after rain, looking for my house,
finding it, all the windows open, books open
to all my favorite pages. What can I say
for my own clatter down Agate Way? Nothing.
I just breathe mist.
Even the dead Christmas tree on my yard looks pretty.
There's nothing we can do about the heart.

# I

# Doctor in the House of the Goddesses

She leans over and breathes into
your face for luck. Both
her earlobes hold fat turquoise studs.
From the folds of her gown
she pulls needle & syringe.
Like the barefoot Chinese doctor
she keeps tincture & sweet oils
in her pockets.
Her hair is black,
held back with ivory combs.
If she could she would
tack your uterus onto the wall
like a medicine pouch,
wring it dry of blood & tissue,
then soak it in a basin of tears.
She will offer you an apple.
Suck it until the skin breaks
and you taste the tart juice.
She will say, "Now I am entering,"
and somehow
you will open for her.
She will say, "Your body is growing
warmer, now, for a moment,"
and you will calculate the time with her.
You will open to her finicky rhythm
of needle & sponge. She will suck you
dry, her silver needle making tracks
inside the hollow arm of your vagina.
Her hands are the center
around which your body stretches & winces.
She says, "Thirty more seconds,"
and her lips whiten.

Twenty-eight seconds pass and she is finished.
Sweat drips from your breasts onto the floor.
You are free.
She packs her sack and as you whisper
your thanks, she goes away
into the next room,
knowing the perfect timing of pain.

# Palomas Fountain

*for Eva Forest, tortured & imprisoned
under Franco. While in prison, she wrote
letters about the healing powers of the
imagination for her children*

I do not know
the scratch of keys
following me into sleep,
or the faces of sullen men
standing over me, holding
me against the steel table
with prods & claws.
I know

the black sockets of my
grandmother's eyes, but
they leave me alone now.
I see them only when
driving late at night, knots
in trees
or birds sleeping
on phone wires.

I know my father
all his hair gone, skin
turned gray in four weeks,
the chemo pursing his mouth
& hands. He's quiet now,
all our old wars are over.
He tells me poetry isn't so
different from welding:
you shield your eyes too long from the blue flame
you can't shape the iron.

"The imagination intervenes in reality and changes it."
I'm happy when I'm working & dreaming at the same time.
Last night my lover dreamed
a giant kangaroo ran past him
down a steep hill
so close he could have touched
that soft gray face.
The pouch, as far as he could see,
was empty;
but he's smiling about pounding hooves
& a heart beating loudly as his.

Childless, I know the blank page
is the only way to reach my children.
The day Franco's men took you
a journey began. "Imagination is a kind
of motor—it moves, and it moves other things.
Sometimes, when I'm thirsty, I stop by the Palomas
Fountain (that is, the white plastic jug
on my bedside table, which I've called
after the doves in my dreams)."

There is a dull sleep
after the lover leaves
and a wait like something you could have written
but didn't try—
Living, then, must be
a blending of two lives:
The white dove beckons and we fly.
Then it gets dark
and the lights click on.

# Motel, on the Anniversary of the Death of John Belushi

David Letterman has the Fabulous Thunderbirds
& a man who can't sleep and never has. He paints
seascapes on the heads of pins. I've locked myself
into a room like the one Belushi died in
after a woman he could barely see
made love to him or drew whatever distinct
pleasure prepared him for death.
I think of her shooting him up and realize
the sharpshooters on the roof of the White House tonight
are robots with their minds on one thing and one thing
only. Just like I can't worry too long about anything
but my insomnia & parade of anxieties:
maybe the burglars have returned to my house,
maybe my brother hurt himself with the chainsaw.
I know this is the result
of heightened sensitivity to

the great pain that surrounds us.
I still ask my uncle to tell the story
of digging his own grave in the War.
Without my asking, my mother tells
how her mother, in the last week of her life,
said, "On Monday, I knew the little death was coming."
It was: her body shriveled except for her
huge ankles swollen with her body's
final treasure. My students cried

the day Belushi died and I didn't understand.
Of course they were crying for themselves.
And more. They cried because

a big laughter burnt itself out. If a life
is small as this room,
it's also loud as a seascape
crashing or breaking or winding up
even in miniature
and all alone.

# Meteorite

I watch my father
breathing in the hospital bed
the kind of bed
a boy or girl
sleeps in alone
waiting for parents
to come home
after a party
opening the door
restoring heat
to the house
with their happiness
I watch the fence
around the bed
that keeps him
from falling out
Under one sky
we fall
when we're sick
or lovestruck

In the dark house
where I grew up
while my father worked
7 days and slept 7 nights
my mother
sleeps alone tonight

while his hard breathing
swells his body
and I have time to notice

my heart whose heat
is hidden like the heat
inside the meteorite, small treasure
from my childhood on the shelf
in my dark house tonight
under one sky
where things fall down
for us, bright and whole

# To Hera

When an apprentice gets hurt, or
complains of being tired, the workmen
and peasants have this fine expression:
"It is the trade which is entering his
body."
— Simone Weil

The silver figure-eights of the Smithfield Street Bridge
rest like giant earrings above the gray river.
Hera, your statues tucked away in the Mellon museums,
like your stories — festival, midnight, magic —
have nothing to tell the homeless.

I see three women
outside the Bethlehem Haven Soup Kitchen.
One pulls at her hair, lugs a bag of bread.
In the huddle of the second
against the warm brick wall
I see my grandmother, bent over,
one breast cut off after the first cancer,
dressing in the dark apartment above the wooden bridge
old cars & workers creaked across
going home every night.
The third woman, heavily pregnant,
has no coat, hat or gloves.
I praise their chapped hands,
I touch their streets,
I want a way to speak.

Hera, protector of women,
take the bridges and bend them
into a bracelet of three golds:
white for the sky turning to ash,
yellow for the sunset,

rose for the glisten on my legs
after love. Renew me as virgin
once each year.
Protect us in our great thirsts.

Because we die and lose everything,
I honor you quietly
with wine & oil, chopped olives
in the black skillet.
I think of Weil
harvesting grapes in the Rhone, in 1941,
how she held up her end of the work,
clumsy with fatigue & hunger
in the long afternoons of white heat.
She worked hard not for ego or forgiveness,
but to touch other lives,
to work her clumsy fingers,
and when she stopped and rested,
held herself, rooted & still.

# My Grandmother's Rags

My grandmother watched for Louie the huckster
& the potato sacks he saved for her,
wrappings for boxes sent to the town I couldn't
pronounce, *Rzeszow*, east of Krakow.
The work took all day,
sewing rags around the box edges,
then the sewing of the name.
Grandmother's fine spidery hand
moved across the address square
fifteen stitches per inch.

My grandmother came from the old country
and sent back dresses with plastic belts,
delicate rayon scarves, packets of coffee
& Camels tucked into white shoes.
For herself she saved the paper from bread,
jar lids & rubber bands. Her daily work
began with rags. Menstrual rags for her
daughters even after bleaching bore sepia
clouds, and clouds of steam lifted as she pressed
rags for the bed for whatever she coughed up
during the night.

She loved anything paisley,
& cheesecake from Rhea's Bakery & the tissue
around the cake which she kept beside clove
& cinnamon & the good rags.
I saw her use only one,
the lace handkerchief
on weddings & the hot, bad days,
wrapped around a potato, arthritis medicine,
for its fresh magic.

# Spring Poem

Tonight fills up
with MTV & weary detours
around the city's broken bridges,
stale bar scenes with everybody's knives out
against public displays of affection.
I want to forget nothing
about watching everybody break up
and praying it's not me next.
There's something to be praised
in charcoal gray weather like this
when it storms each morning,
fogs over from noon to two,
then opens to a blue skybowl around five.
Jackson Browne & new potatoes
are here for us.
So are white plum blossoms
snowing on the yard & settling
in your hair.
So are artichokes & DiPrima &
frascati chilling on the back porch.
Like the old river woman who died alone
hoping to return in her next life as a lizard,
let me curl up in the dark, damp places
so I might lose those places again
as this week turns into next,
as tonight turns into morning & you
opening the door.

# To the Female Rockstars, 1985

Most weekends
I'm in a hundred-year-old bar
at a corner table with friends, coffee & beer.
Tonight all the performer has
is a bright red guitar, a half dozen songs
& a new haircut carefully slicked back.
She wears an earcuff & a purple braid,
checks the crowd for her lover.
Her voice like her song is plain
but it's got a low bite.
She's singing about a job gone wrong
& a woman who wants her child back.
I wonder what Madonna's sugary whine really wants
though what we women want we have to want
a little harder. I'm not giving up on
sheer electronic thrill, I'm going to

risk it, stars, and tell you the truth:
I have tickets for next Saturday night
to see the greatest woman rock guitarist in the world.
I'll be the one in the ninth row back,
foot on my imaginary distortion box
as June Millington plugs in
who twenty years ago with her sister Jean
started an all-woman band called Fanny
that played the poorer clubs
and when it got press got Barbarella
treatment. A twenty-year-old guitar player
I saw on a LIVE AID commercial said:

"If you aren't honest about
rock and roll people can sense it."

I'm talking about the guitar
& a woman whose arm moves like a cobra,
whose voice contorts like her face,
whose story moves all the way up
from her hips and you hear it,
stars, when you come down off the charts
just this once. Come down and listen,
come down and play.

# *To Simone Weil*

after reading two contemporary poets
who declare that "self-knowledge" and
"a clear sexual identity" would have
saved her


Had you forgotten god & a wild curiosity
you may have lived past 34,
beyond exhaustion & a sparse diet.

In Florida, in the glittering heat
five women try
to cover themselves,
burned, freezing,
as they run from the abortion clinic
bombed by terrorists.
In Bonn, a woman fighting pornography
lifts the Bic lighter, ignites herself.
She bursts, red & orange blossom
in a parking lot.
Abstinence, or swimming or dreaming nonstop
all are choices we make, if we're lucky.

You could have bought more time
and we would have more now to hold & read.
But I feel your wish
driving ahead of me like a haywagon.
You held onto private life & public study
that stepped out of its apartment one morning,
small suitcase in hand, and disappeared,
keeping and losing your family,
touching friends only through letters
in the middle of your work, always your work.
If you suffered, hardly a wisp of smoke appeared.

When I open any of your books
to almost any page
and the words skitter like tiny birds
then focus magically like the *I Ching*
I begin, alone at my desk, to see
many things, faces, to see myself
and what you said we're here for: beauty,
like a sphinx, like the land fragrant
at harvest, silent & tantalizing.

# Sara's Terrace

Thirty-five minutes from Rome
I could name all her herbs in Italian:
*basilico, rosmarino* like names of the
church ladies who would nurse her that winter;
the thick bronchitis would finally kill her
three hundred days from that day; she came out

from the four cool rooms,
watering can balanced on a tray,
steel braid coiled around her nape.
Blue-green tiles framed the trellis,
peach roses just touched her hair as she walked
the tiny walkway in the sun.

"So, still the same president in America?"
"So, your garden, you still scratch like a chicken?"
And she led me to a huge clay pot
spilling oregano stalks laden with the soft green buttons.
She knew the bus stop,
the corner drugstore, three neighbors & the church.
I was the last from America to see her
alive, I counted: seven children, eighty years,
three sugars in her espresso, two petals
stuck to her black silk stocking.

## Wildsisters Bar

How do you operate a jackhammer if
you've never owned a toolbox?
Who knows how to vent a stinking drain?
Those questions and the pleasing ones —
can we invite the Roches
to do a gig soon? —
pound at us while we build fire walls, sand chairs, replace wiring.
The unemployed guitarist who lives upstairs
solemnly agrees that Neil Young is the father of punk.
We move on to Grace Jones,
Grace Slick. May the mother of punk
be with us forever,
her fierce & beautiful curls
forever in our faces.
Neighborhood men drop by the hundred-year-old
building while we work, give us the raised fist.
How's the *sisterhood* going? Slowly. According
to Rita, who hasn't seen a paycheck in 90 days
and works this project between bus trips to the
welfare line, the work is moving.

.   .   .

The trauma nurse wheels Rita into surgery for the fifth time. No one
is saying why was she out so late and why was she out so late
in a place like that. Because her swollen body, filled with the yellow
sap of infection, is something even we don't recognize.

.   .   .

If I could I'd call de Beauvoir or Leduc and say
things haven't changed much.
Store windows fill up with plastic

women-corpses, mouths pursed in false horror,
legs parted as if dreading that which
in breathless joy
might open them further.
99 percent of the women on MTV
are half-dressed & half-witted.
We want art
for those on the brink
of finding a place to speak,
who want
desire
that short-
circuits the voicebox.

   .   .   .

Only the hum of the ice machine
& the quiet bubble of soup,
Lee's hair turning to silk
under the stagelights.
On this, the night before opening
I'm happy as the girl who
turned back her bedcovers
and found nothing but roses,
happy as I dream of Dana
lost in a tub of bubbles & herbs
after long days & no time
for bathing or sweet sleep.
Happy we're all on fine tuning
waiting for the slow pulse of music,
the clink & glisten of glasses,
the faces shining at the door.

   .   .   .

Rita, returned from death
with one strong leg,
my friends in your patience & wit,

here are tools we need:
two, or six voices in agreement, encouragement
when one voice hears no answer;
the heavy bucket of nails
the neighborhood men left by the door for us,
the kettle boiling its resistance in the 50-degree room,
simple things, some large, though,
like loneliness,
like the grip of a hand saying goodbye,
the face greeting us at the door
falling off its hinges.

# Moving to New York

*for Gilbert*

When you get there, walk into the Cafe Deutschland,
not the painting by Jorg Immendorf, but a bar I'm imagining
and the cold will leave you like a jacket dropped to the floor
before a blazing fire, orange ceiling, blue walls,
a green leather floor still warm from the women
getting up to leave (not on your account; they're off
to another party). Order a drink, hot & strong; everybody looks
ready, their clean hair & thick sweaters breathing at you,
and the paintings are amazing: a country scene folds in on itself
forever, its tiny scale happy & intricate, like you.

The night you left
you joined a long list of expatriates,
all my old friends gone to California
or East. Industry was dead ten years ago
and our country of two classes, one called *retrain*,
and the other *acquire*, moves on, wobbly & mean.
You stretch into a future, funneling canvases in
from Germany (another country in need of a culture).
The young Expressionists want to meet you.
They have. They're happy they're painting and making
money & small businesses and talking about
where they buy their jeans. And they make good art!
About your one worry—you'll survive as an organism
in the big streets & small greeneries.
The morning coffee tastes good as you ride
up the elevator, and when you ride down at night
the steel doors open, the great glass doors
of the building hush closed, and you walk into
the avenue, the city silver & black
as your eyeglasses & coat.

# Sheila's Flat

Stencils everywhere: ducks, trees, demitasse
cups, a window she knocked out with a sledgehammer,
smaller & larger versions of that window stenciled
on every available foot of ceiling & loft

and a giant hookah with mouthpieces that look
like nipples, though all the girls tell her it's
politically incorrect to call them that

and in the kitchen Sheila is heating milk
for coffee and working on a new canvas & video
simultaneously and I am in the bathroom checking
her latest reading material including the Greenfield
Green Tab & Gemology Journal and her preserved copy

of the manifesto that demanded tampax—
Free to All People—at every Turnpike
entrance & exit, and I am looking
out her window onto the South Side

& her garden which after rain
radiates out like a map of Paris
but whose beds are named

Silvermound Artemesia
Violet Way
Avenue of the Lobelia

# *Fabian*

was to Elvis
as Travolta is to Springsteen
is to
Rock itself,
and my brothers said
he was gay,

but I forgot I was 16 & too old to care
one night in a pizzeria in Montclair, 1967.
I was in love with the boys
at the counter
whose wet black hair
curled over their
white shirt collars. They handled
the slender bottles of olive oil,
talked on the phone, joked & sang
to each other in Sicilian
thick & bronze as their fingers & lips.
I practiced a dangerous
& hopeless look
and stepped up to the counter
of the True Italy, far from Pittsburgh
& its ignorance of classic lust
and I wanted those boys

as much as I wanted Fabian
& his voice on the box and I was
on top of him, pretty greaser,
his hands grabbing me around the waist

tossing me into the air high above
the tight olives & discs of pepperoni
sweating in their steel bins and I
flew, with Fabian, the palms of our hands
sticky with flour & spice.

## Smoking Cigars with Li Po

There must be a way I can lose everything by throwing myself
on the floor and untying my kimono, or, better yet, having it untied

by one of your dancing girls—where are they? I remember the one
with dark hair who kissed me and said, "You're always kvetching

about something and you don't know what you want," and I didn't but
I'm burning faster than ever, I'm writing the poem, I tilt

my eyebrows to the angle of the room and squint you to the typewriter
voluptuous & blunt as grappa. You unwrap two Garcia y Vegas, teach me:

the secret of the inhale is to forget everything since adolescence.
You say, "I didn't know *that*!" when I tell you about Che &

de Beauvoir. You speak Turkish & Jamaican & pure talk I haven't
heard much since 1969. I'm learning the secret of photographic

memory. I already know the patience of the Iron Goddess, at least
I think I do since I'm in love with at least two dreams at a time

and I don't believe in coded language, I want to wander like you,
crazy uncle, home on my back. I don't believe in, say, Gertrude

Stein's baby sleeping in white eyelet in her perfect garden. I only
see Alice emptying the diaper pail again. I'm more interested in

Amy Lowell's cigars & the penis for its own sake and—hey—give me
some fingers & knees & lips I can do some serious work with, & time

because time is hot hot as the match I strike now and raise to my lips.
Why you, Li Po, so far and so close? Whatever it is we might have in common

is our crookedness, you, bent over a waterfall, singing, & me,
leaning over Turtle Creek, looking for crayfish, looking for my

Level Green, which was not level but was so green I thought
the Earth dropped off at the crest of my hill where the trees

waved like plumes against the cobalt universe. If it's true
that you went out while trying to grasp the moon

then I'll hang the full moon of my childhood over you
and I'll stand up and keep on taking the test and

I'll wash this floor only to dance on it all night & day
long, my hair going up in smoke.

# II

# The Polish Blouses

Aniela says, "Eat!" and I slide bread
& scallions onto my plate. I'll never
be able to say the hard "r" or softly
tongued "l." She smiles in memory
of my sad & moody grandmother whom she
hugged goodbye at Gdansk. She speaks
little because I've come home only to leave
so soon. I count five rolls of Kennedy halves
for my cousins, twenty-five fives for their parents.
She asks what I've seen in Paris.
The paintings of Georges de la Tour.

She has saved meat from last weekend
for my visit. Some kielbasa, a slice
of ham, greasy & hard. The paintings,
she says. The candles looked real
and so did the fruit on the plates,
I tell her. She lines up a row of glasses.
Vodka. I don't drink it, but the way she
nods, I drink. I give her the coins,
she gives me stamps, two medals from the
Prussian Army & her last school photograph.
In 1909 she was eight years old

and this is where she worked
the rest of her girlhood: log house,
straw roof, mud floors. In 1909
she told her teacher she wouldn't be back.
"I fold up my shoes in paper
and go to the door. He stop me and say
'And what will you do the rest of your life

but dig in dirt and clean after cows.'
He wipe his eyes with tears."

Aniela Lorens leads me over the Little Wisloka,
feet steady on the thin log.
She snaps off the chicken's neck
and her breasts jump lightly.
Germans came during the first war
for her potatoes & cellar of vodka.
At the foot of the great bed, in the great trunk,
quilts & blouses pressed against each other,
all the stitches winding like tiny streams of tears
while she gave birth. The stitches wound like creeks
where she fished in her countryside
as beautiful as her sister's Pennsylvania.
The soldiers set up camp on the stoop.
They trampled the garden but never
touched the woman whose braid curled
around her neck like a snake.
She snaps the chicken's neck.
I snap the laundered blouses from the line.

Now like dancers they wrap me
in red & purple flowers & knotted leaves.
Their sleeves are simple wings.
Their collars white birds sleeping
near my tanned face. I keep them
beside my old blue workshirt & good
white dress. Undressing for bed,
I catch myself in the mirror, touch my blouse
to the dome of her forehead. Now I'm
cool enough for a good night's sleep.

# Father's Magic Trick

He could grab the hot casserole and dance
the kitchen with it while we clapped
and squealed at him never to put it down.
"I have hot hands," he'd sing and laugh
at supper in the early Sixties
when I pretended I was the meteor girl

who stood beside him leaning over the pool
inside the nuclear dome where he worked
adjusting fuelrods like pickup sticks
to stoke the fire that meant
heat, light & wealth for us all.

He worked with his hands tying
fuel bundles in the chambers of Fermi & Chalk River.
His hands were thick as oven mitts,
safe enough after touching the atomic fire
to touch anything. Down in the cellar
welding toys & lawnchairs bare-handed
he always had an audience at the window,
kids peering in at the strobes
watching him bend over his
blue flame & wand.

## The Man in the Gray House

Of course they said
he died of loneliness, a broken heart
three months after his mother passed,
though they also said
they feared he
did things to children,
lured them up onto the silken
gray boards of his porch
and inside behind the
gray lace curtains.

Walking from school
I saw him in the window
and he looked so sad
he scared me, my own
long face
big chin
something like his
pressed to the glass.

I saw him outside once
watering his roses,
the white flowers leaning
their faces up to his,
the factory in the background
tossing up its ribbons of smoke.

My girlfriend said
she & her mother, the visiting nurse,
had gone in there.
He had soup cooking on the stove
& big carrot discs & celery stalks

laid out on the kitchen table
oilcloth that had red roosters on it.
She said his eyes were red
all around the rims
and that he cried when they left,
begged them
to stay for supper,
for Lawrence Welk,
for the six o'clock news,
for anything
they wanted.

## The Lightning Girl

enters my dreams again
telling me what she saw
the night of the storm: the fireball

big as a tomato
smashed her bed. Afterward,
head & hair alive with electricity, she sat
in the open window on the cold sill

talking to herself all night, the dark green
spring storm raining in on her,
rain sliding off the roof of the porch

where she hung with the neighborhood boys
summer nights checking me out
when I made my long walk up the boring street.

While she napped near the creek
I was in the woods sleeping
under the Great Elm; when she came looking

I took off up into a tree above Roundtop
invisible to everyone but her down there
in the gold weeds, burning herself in

like a meteor. She was
Janey    Shinya    White Fox
all the invented names hissing

like things we whispered to each other
under my sheets. I spelled her name
in lipstick on my bedroom wall. I stole

the chocolate cake for her, I stole my mother's
rouge, unscrewed the cap, tilted the bottle
over the white bed: the drawing wobbled

across the sheet—it's a house and Janey
& I are in it. The silver skybowl
hovers over us, charges us, we want to be

artists. We whisper the word and nearly
see it
razoring the sky.
She pulls me down on top of her
and we wrestle till we're hot
& scratched. My gypsy stands in for me
when the caravan of parents arrives.
She lies for me.
She lies down in purple phlox
waiting for me.
She empties every mailbox on our street,
we open the letters, bills & magazines
so I'll learn to read.
We smoke every night
coughing so hard
our laughs blow out
every match. Our voices tap the night
like woodpeckers,
we live in a treehouse
with shale & feathers,
crayfish & tadpoles
& the little box of meteorites
we hide like stolen babies.
We know babies
are something too terrifying to make—
we know this the way we know
how to hide here forever, or
how to leave and never come back.

How she survived the fireball,
no one ever knew.
How she ended up
living on the road ten years
no one knew. She sends me roses,
her eyes follow me
to Paris, from Thailand
where she sweeps temple steps
and learns za-zen.

I'm writing at a frozen picnic table
surrounded by burnt gold fields
& crows big as black tablecloths.
What I've become is
more of a haunt
seeking out forsaken places
where I might be struck

like a bird zagging
like a black bolt
in a sky silvered with promises.

# Troy Hill Voices

I want my father to forget the river,
the dark room & the priest
wiping the girl's body
with the cool white cloth.

The twenty upright stones
in the ten-foot-square plot
are rock silhouettes
on a fuchsia sky. But he says
he's tired of listening
to their sad voices.
When we walk among his dead
in any weather, his voice
is the only warm thing.

I want him to forget
walking the river's curve
past Herrle's Dairy
with buckets of milk,
spoiled milk
for his sister who died
as he watched from the doorway.

*2.*

This stone, the tall one,
is cousin Kathleen's, age sixteen,
sent to her room for smoking in public.
And her leap, in white nightgown,
from the third floor window
above Herr's Island where pigs & livestock
were pushed like a brown river

uphill to the slaughterhouse
just past her door.

When I was sixteen
in my father's house
we argued everything:
the waste-heated river &
its mutant fish, his old argument
that nature can adapt to anything.
I shrilled out our losses
like a strange bird
colliding with a chainsaw.
I wanted an absolute current
of joined lives.

3.

Now we walk among our dead
and try to learn to talk.
He's mesmerized by houselights
across the river, sending him
messages like beams
from distant caves.
In this graveyard I can't see or hear
anything, but I know memory
is radioactive, and so are the river
& the tiny cluster of swimmers
who splash below Troy Hill
in the glinting brown water.

Where Herrle's Dairy stood
my father sees his dead sister:
"There she is. I see her
running in the field. Her hair is blond."
He wants to brush her hair
and listen to her, he wants to sing to her
while sweat like fresh rain
cools her face.

# Music Lessons

My mother packed me off to music school in May
and the college girls wore white gloves.
Sister Ann Agnes said:
"No, don't look at *me*. Don't look at your hands.
Close your eyes. Listen and you'll hear it."
She sang a high, bird note. I listened,
my eyes gliding over light pools on the wall.
Notes were everywhere,
secret as the girls' voices out on the lawn.
I found high F sharp. She smiled,
giving me the first perfect thing
I'd ever known.

Now she sang her mellowest note,
its tremolo breathing across the top of my hair.
She leaned toward the open window
and the vibrato curled into my spine.
I watched sprinklers wave
like silver harps. I played
a simplified Debussy,
my fingers skinny birds over water,
the water rising
like mist above the keys.

## The Boy Who Sat in the Barber's Lap

After school
we sneaked past the door
always slightly open,
in order to hear
Clyde & the boy laughing.
It wouldn't have mattered if anyone
bold enough had walked in on the man,
his lips slightly parted, hands moving
up the boy's thighs
which looked to me round & alive
in my town where nothing happened
except to this boy whose concentration
was absolute, looking up into the man's
face, their faces round & strained,
wild as I was in my girlfriend's arms
ringed with dirt, hidden in bluebells.
The boy was my age
and knew he was special in his life
so charged with his
absence from us. Fragrant oils & bottles
of scent framed the mirrors, & reflections there
in the dangerous moments before sex.
In my girl's arms,
*You be the boy*, I'd say, arms pinned behind my head.
We took turns
while the trees
moved, making their sounds.
I was the girl who stared all summer
from my grandmother's porch;
I stared into the blouse
of the teenage mother, her kids
peeking from the hedges. Her breasts

were peach, nipples like pale cones.
The boy missed school and
was frequently ill. He & Clyde
dressed alike and held hands
walking the suburban roads.
We shunned him, listened to our parents:
Pay no attention.
*Are you talking to me? I haven't seen anything.*

## The Girl Who Fed Her Dog Bolts

carried a trashcan lid for a shield
in street fights I watched
from our kitchen window

threw a football before most of us
figured out how to hold one

lived in a cement foundation.
(her dad too poor to finish the house).

I was sent one Saturday to help
with homework: a story of a woman
stoned to death in a lottery;
the girl said she'd read it
and liked the ending.

She'd gotten her period before any of us
and knew how the blood flowed
and how the pains were nothing
and all the paraphernalia nothing
but trouble
and tossed her Kotex belt on the table
like a jockstrap.

She had beautiful hair
with a widow's peak
my mother took as a sign
she'd grow up to be
glamorous & rich.
In her treehouse she kept
silk scarves she'd bought at Goodwill.

She tied them to my wrists & ankles,
showed me how to do the princess dance.

The teachers whispered
after her dad left
and her mother took in boarders
during hunting season. I knew
they knew about the bulldog, too

his jowls shaking,
tail wagging, tongue
lapping each silver nugget
from her hand.

He loved whatever she fed him,
supper scraps, oranges, sassafras
leaves & the bolts she rationed
from her toolbox.
He lived the good life, let us
dress him up
carry him up to the treehouse
and watched us dance,
the full weight of him
precious in his princess' loft.

# Where We Came From

### Game

His boots clomping up the steps
to the bedroom. His sister & I
taking turns hiding in the closet
of doll dresses, old sweaters oozing cologne.
One of us waiting for him on the bed.
His hair imitation Elvis,
his pants tight, face red when
he climbed on top of me and
counted to ten. His cock
hidden in his jeans, but I didn't know
anything but my brother's baseball cup,
or guns, or running & locking
the bathroom door. He pushed us,
screaming into the closet while he
disappeared and came back to do it
all over again. We held our breath,
chilled, waiting for their mother
to climb the stairs.

### Cousin

Dziekuje (thank you), and dobra noc (good night),
and we went up to bed. Past Grandpa
weaving down the steps, and Grandma lining his boots
with newspaper. Past the aunt's bedroom, slowly,
listening for the radio's accordion & bass.
We opened the venetian blinds and striped the wall.
My cousin was fragrant with
root beer & potato chips, the woods.
Dozing into the forest of sleep
I held a girl whose braids were
tight & shining, like mine.

# Home Wake

We are so small
all we know is tables — card tables,
kitchen tables carried in, carried out,
Grandmother's house rearranged.
The old Polish soldiers plan the walk
to the cemetery, the old musicians
smoke cigars, wait to eat,
their accordion cases black
as our fathers' boxy suits.

Uncle, you are our big doll,
we sneak you fists of violets
from the backyard where the keg
sticks up out of its silver tub
stuffed with ice. Our hands are cold,
we touch your shoulder and talk
to you, though all you know of English
is work, tv & whiskey.
All the Sunday foods pile up
on the sideboard. We play
at the hems of our aunts' aprons
while they carve ham.
The guests want to eat, we eat
our kielbasa, wipe our mouths.
Yours, pink & gray, is smiling.
Death hasn't made his way
through the guest line yet.
In your coffin you look
small enough to tend
but too big to lift out.
After you leave

we play Heinz factory
out back in the yews, separate
the green leaves, red berries
while our dolls lounge
in their shade and watch us work.
We sort, pack, stack our foods.
We love the smear mud makes
on the alley bricks,
wipe our hands on toby leaves,
clean our shoes with spit.

# Feast Day

Having scrubbed the sinks with Comet, the bronze stains
dissolved like years, having swept the front & back
steps, lit the stove and plunked the turkey
onto the crooked rack, having bundled the newspapers
and burned them, having removed Uncle Stanley's corpse
from the diningroom table where its aura & warnings
have remained these 30 years since our mothers &
grandmothers were in charge, we take charge,
send up one prayer to St. Jude, saint of the gold

disc that hung from my mother's neck while she tried
to conceive me, and another to the friendly ghosts
who survived McCarthy the way we're surviving Reagan-Bush
and one more to the cats & squirrels in the battle
at the window which isn't really a battle but a dance
whose messages etch speed & stealth onto the scratched
glass. Saints of lost causes, we're ready for you
on this day with thick wine & clean dishes

having tuned our music to the sound of boots coming up
the steps and going down so many nights of plotting & talking
not about the revolutions that haven't come, but the
twists that enable them, having listened for the millionth time
to "Time Is On My Side," having danced hard enough
to warm up. Our muscles stretch and the table is
heavy & steaming as the table we sat around during the Fifties

when we were nieces & little sisters & our parents'
little pink stars, scrubbed and stuffed between the grownups'
laughs & conversations. There was a quiet over America then as now
and I wonder if there's something building again
under the whirr of helicopters & guns,

the country torn between the news & the Super Bowl.
I hear my mother at the end of the Sixties:
"You can't feed the whole world. You'll see, you'll feel the
same way some day." But I don't. And I hear her saying
"The family isn't just the family" as she made room for another
face at her table, and another, and in this season of old
friends returning, reconciliations honored though we no longer
need them, I sit down with my friends, having unpacked
the holiday lamps & dancing scarves one more winter night.

# Lavenders

Who knew what was happening when
I bent down to the green leaves
hiding my face after I first saw
the muscles in her
sunburnt shoulders?

.   .   .

The almondate leaves
swollen as her lips
bitten from my kiss

.   .   .

The scent couldn't have been strong
as turpentine
but it stung me that way
the summer I was so drunk
after loving her
I painted the kitchen walls blue as lavender
blue as my oldest workshirt,
the one that fits perfectly
when I wear it open

.   .   .

The showers are so cold at camp
my scalp throbs, and when I walk, afterward,
into the forests of lovers,
Diana & her secret animals
welcome me in

.   .   .

Thick homegrown leaves
dropped into the bath,
thick Spanish oil
smeared on the back seat
of her car.

.    .    .

The silk ribbon I lace around the wrist
of the bronze Athena, nine feet tall.
I stand before her
beautiful square toes & feet,
look up into her eyes
and she looks back.

.    .    .

The tattoo I don't have—
a slice of purple moon
just below my left knee;
her face on it

# III

## Looking for Level Green

Seneca once told a white man
the way to Fort Duquesne was
"West. Two days through forest.
Then cross a long, level green."

Now a suburb of the suburb of
Monroeville, home of the nondestructive
Nuclear Facility. No uranium on site.
No plutonium. No more blue collars.

Ten minutes, though, and you're in a green
pocket called Daugherty's Grove
where my parents fell in love
and where bluebells drift behind gaspumps
standing sentinel to a sad forest of dwarves.

Ten minutes from the fat cool mall & condos
framing the thruway
stands Roundtop, old burial mound, ignoring
anyone's wishes to dig bones or potsherds or memories.
A girl can lie down there and not think, for once.

And ten minutes from the weapons site
that has no dripping, leaking
or raw oily places
slouches the Shades of Death
where a woman killed herself for love.
There's nothing but
dark pines down in there
alive and holy, alive with her.

# Doris Lash

had more books than anyone
we knew, & sheet music &
a piano that faced Roundtop.
My lessons drifted out
through the mended screens
the day I threw up
all over the keys—
a secret anxiety or summer flu—
but Doris cooed over me, cleaned me
and sat down to play
something melodic & stormy,
while I dozed on her couch.
She played as if to say
the only upheavals worth having
are those that turn you upside down.

I am so in love
thirty years later:
all I wanted for my birthday this morning
was a cold beer & my lover's jeans
thrown on my floor and I got both.
Tonight my radio plays
Irish music which fusses over hedges
& daylilies so I lift one finger to
turn the dial and down that winding path

Doris is playing
while supper burns on her woodstove
and her dishes pile up.
I know she was the angel in her house,
and looked like Woolf, but softer.
Her hands were red from weeding &

three sons whose shirts always showed
stitches carefully retraced in the elbows.
And now she's telling me to
go ahead. An angel is picking up socks,
answering my mail . . . I go ahead,
lie here on the couch, indulge myself.
I brood and rest and nothing
interrupts while she plays and plays for me.

# Your Beauty Book, *1961*

Don't wear a raincoat
when it isn't raining

Don't use your nails
if you want them to grow

Keep your tools in a totable basket
The stores are full of cute gadgets

How do you look
in class or at the office?

Any American girl worth her salt
can look like a living doll

Happiness can do it: have you ever
seen an ugly bride?

Censor your meals ahead of time
Now, in winter, is time to get ready

You can't make up in a day
for weeks of neglect

You're at the top where your brains are
Fill in the corners of your lips

Sheila's prize was
a makeover by Kenneth of Lilly Daché

Grace combs beer through her bangs
Haven't you wished a miracle could happen?

Remove the little belt loops from a dress
they spoil a clean waistline

Before buying hairspray
decide what you want to do with it

How do you look at the office?
Moody? Fight it out with other interests

Describe yourself *Time* magazine style:
Would you be "pudgy, casual Ethel Smith?"

If you must be a one-coat girl
why not decide you like the age you are?

Suppose your hair is bodiless
Stores are full of cute gadgets

The beehive & artichoke
won Sheila her trip

The First Lady's headdress
says *Grecian* & *sleek*

Every time you eat
check your lipstick

Eliminate by experiment
How do you pay for it all?

Proper bag & underwear
contribute their perfect fit

Stores are full of cute gadgets
metal-bound, unbreakable

pretty enough for a dressing table
If you need a girdle with your "best" clothes

you probably need one most of the time
Date coming in half an hour? Try

Cherries in the Snow
Fire and Ice

## Watching the James Wright Video
## in Martins Ferry, Ohio

This morning in the library's "other room"
the guest poets labored over
"How do I know if I'm a poet?"
and "Why should I write if I know I'm going to die?"
and "Who do you save, the drowning poet, or the poems?"
then singers from Cleveland gave
an operatic rendition of "Just off the highway to Rochester, Minnesota";
at the book sale I picked up a pretty copy
of the *Rubáiyát* and Frank got a City Lights book
for a quarter.

"Get your feet off the chair,"
the nervous old woman says to Ann.
The screen flickers, he looks
shy & plain as one of my uncles.
The old woman is
aunt of the poet
who "never got to see Jim at the end
so I wanted to see this."
We watch the right hand
push the glasses up on his nose
and light another cigarette mid-poem.
An Ohioan behind us says
"Yeah, we like his poems,
except the one about the whorehouse."

Nothing now but the voice, Appalachian resin
and pear blossoms & the Italian evening.
The voice carries me to the railroad tracks
picking violets all afternoon.

I'm lost in the purple flowers.
I press them into his book,
into poems all the way to Venice
where sisters & brothers calmly
brush their hair in the gold dusk.

# Poem Beginning with a Line from Hemingway

Do not start blaming who you love

the world of bombs & fear
does enough that's bad

We leave the house at two a.m.
for the dark street and I wonder
how long it takes to start a war
and if tonight
the president will feel sick enough
to do it

We walk and suddenly I notice
the birds beginning spring
but they sound like the screeking
voices of my grandmothers
warbling over the phone, sending
their messages of complaint

"Are those birds or people?" I ask you
and you tell me

this is the way they sound in spring
ragged throats & chirping horns
released into the galaxy
marking the equinox
and breaking time
They don't know what control is and if they did
they wouldn't want it     I want to lose

the control the last strands of winter
hold over us, webs of fatigue from work
& 27 days straight of no sun

and I want to say
that time I was angry at you
and hurt
I gave it up because

crabapples, when I was a girl,
were sweeter than I was,
crying over everything, even
the color of my blouse on any given
Saturday afternoon

Who wants that kind of sour?
When you were off *somewhere with her*
I was probably
off happy
under stars
anyway

I believe
in you
& birds that hug the updraft
in their dark charcoal perfect lines
so fast we barely see flashes of black
under the streetlamps. Passing the Seven-Eleven
we read the headlines announcing
the monotony of the president's fear

If tonight I mistake birds
for people it's because I'm in love
with you & birds in updraft always
needing to descend again to the earth
like Neruda's gulls
carrying the letters of the world
& the questions

# Uncle's Home Movies, Troy Hill

Uncle John now dead six months
keeps appearing in Atlantic City,
jerky & delicate, different woman each time
fluttery in flowered dresses & thin-strapped
shoes. Or he's sitting in a corner
of a backyard, looking small at 14 as he did
at 71. The cut to the picnic table
blurs onto a few dishes of food & an army
of plates. It is 1930 and the collage,
all outdoors & vacation, is half the story.
The other half is

his rage,
the one-truck towing business lost
when the unions came in,
Troy Hill house lost, baby brother
dead of convulsion & not enough to eat.
The WPA camps were waystations
for a few cousins, but he
chokes at that too, and

Roosevelt the biggest hoax of the century.
Everything else incoherent:
bodies of the dead surrounded him in the Pacific
seven days after the War was over.
Sometimes he is lost in 1943 in the Aleutians
digging his own grave in July
because by winter the ground will be too hard.
He lifts the pistol
and the dog who will starve
drops to the snow.

Uncle winds up for the pitch, it's wild
and he's hit, he's laughing,
icebag to his forehead in the maple grove
backlit with two o'clock sun.
Now he is smiling, canoeing
with my aunt on their first date

and planting the lilac over the well
he's just dug behind the house
he built in 1949, still new
in its single luxury.

# The Nuclear Accident
# at SL 1, Idaho Falls, 1961

My father remembers a nurse
talking from her hospital bed,
off-limits in her dome, like a ghost
or captured angel, still full of what
she'd managed to do: climb the ladder,
free the man so hot they had to wait
before burying him, till they scraped
his skin and cleaned his bones.
After three weeks she was still alive
and slowly dying, telling the
ridiculous bad luck of it:

A guy's standing, settling the fuel bundle
into the reactor
and his buddy comes up and gooses him.
The bundle jerks, the lid of the great
vessel slides open and off. The guy
is blasted up
impaled to the ceiling
by a shaft of steam & a metal rod
his white-suited body
stuck up there
and no one,
all of them evacuated,
can get him down till
days later the medical team
enters the containment
in jumpsuits & booties.
My father remembers the nurse
entering the dome, pretty & bright.

It takes brilliance to be a heroine
& something secret & stupid.
She walks across the shining floor.
She places her foot on the first rung
then the next, climbs up.
She must know how stupid this is.
It's only a body up there
and the air is invisible
with what will kill her.
Has anyone given her anything to take along
on this trip? Rabbit foot? Heart on a chain?
Can she see anything in the face looking
down at her? She holds herself
up. She pulls him down.
She walks to the ambulance & lead coffin.
She knows what she is doing.
She knows what she has to do.

# The Gesture

The first time I dreamed about the Oak Ridge donkeys
making their circle, brains damaged,
making their circle watched by scientists & tourists
down the road from the plant, I tried to count
them away like sheep. But they couldn't jump
or disappear and I was forced to watch the circle
like a lesson, like my father's gesture

when he was flat on his back sleeping after work.
You wouldn't know he was alive unless you watched
the stretch of his fingers twitching
the air above his chest.
"This is the cleanest work I've ever done,"
he'd say, home from the plant
tight as a vault.

A man he knew
tried filtering contaminated water,
burnt the flesh off the bones
of his fingers. "This is absolutely new,"
my dad would say, designing
controls & loops at the kitchen table.

My father had a strong body when he was young.
A mind like a vault.
He was graceful holding the pencil.
He was happy rising up from sleep.

# Fourteen Nights

The radiator clanks its February chimes
and I'm awake all night with fresh coffee & headphones
feeding me Italian, the one constant aphrodisiac:
*Ecco un'arancia*/here's an orange
and I make my way back to Lodi via the night train
and the weekend all the sailors came aboard carrying
baskets of fruit, salami & olives, sharing it
all with me and I first understood all soldiers
are boys pledged to death. They kissed me and waved
when I got off near my flat above the butcher shop
where sparrows hung by their ankles
and I walked the twenty iron steps up
to my unheated rooms. Above the piazza
whose Romanesque arches curved like bookends
I read all of Lawrence and watched
the Italian presidential elections on tv
fourteen nights straight.

Letters from home
that winter, 1971, with their all-night
sex & refined organic mescaline
made me sick for love. I sat
under the bronze lamp & red blanket
reading the novels and when Birkin ran
into the forest, scraping himself on
branches & rocks I wanted to look into the faces
of all the men I'd never slept with
but thought about and ask
why he did that. The men I knew then
would have said it was his *masculine soul*
uniting with Nature, green & powerful enough
to annihilate everything. Death & joy riveted

Lawrence, but so did unhappy sex, bottled up
& inspected. I figured the Italians
knew better with their screaming & cigars.
They loved the secret ballot & clean white paper.
They loved black coffee & microphones & endless
voting because it meant endless choosing.

At the end of loneliness
I discovered the good poems
& their impossible burn.
I read them on trains passing
the little Autostrada towns, Biella
& Santhia reminding me of all the
Pittsburgh towns Mencken missed
on his train ride through Hell.
The secret mafiosi villages where my uncles
knew which bars gave credit and which ones
opened to the secret knock.
I thought I was different from everybody then,
a woman alone on a train
loneliest woman in the world
burning to make my choices.

## Nursing the Sunburn

Only here that I roll my dope
in banana-flavored papers and sip coffee
with a vibrator salesman. I'm finally
androgynous since I look like Neil Young
in mirrored sunglasses. This is the place
where I could have grown up to be
Isabelle Adjani with smoky eyes
& a body that would never want to wear
anything but black.
There's a baby pelican
on the back porch and Nina Simone's
on the stereo. Motor boats unzipping
the canal cost more than houses do
back home, and some restaurants
can only be reached by water.

The Intercoastal Waterway funnels the aroma
of open sewers,
and backs of ships in Biscayne Bay
are stacked with tractor trailers bearing
bumper stickers like, "I brake for nice tits,"
& "I honk for Jesus." In Miami Beach while rats
scrape across boulders inches from my
bare feet, I'm happy to find
a chunk of white coral and I'm happy
I'm going back to snow & to my own cold house
with firewood stacked up on the porch,
where everything is quiet:
only smoke & the small gray city outside.

# To Wine

Gentle cauldron
in etched glass,
take from the mind
the muzzle of our pasts;
take from love its allegiance to change.
Let us crawl into this garnet cave,
orchard of pomegranates.
Give our blood
the pulse of the evening planet—
Jupiter? So be it.

We're not prepared
for heat in our throats
like the hummingbird's tremblings
while sipping the honey
of a flower thinner than glass.
We love this place where nothing
can happen.

*after Louise Bogan*

## Steven, in His City Garden

Wrecked again, and a rasp from
last night's smoke: there you were
again in the bar gabbing
with women of questionable
attachment and dropping your
bummed Camels in your spilled
beer. But here
are forget-me-nots & cherry-colored
snapdragons whose thick wide chins
drool in this wet July.
Peat moss & sheep manure,
crabgrass & slag
all gifts from the last tenants.
Li Po's book sits on the stoop
humming      It's good to be drunk
on summer     in the morning
and listen to the chirping
of love
as long as this is the day's work.
Your hair is curly
as the tendrils of snow peas, but
it's too late for peas
and the headache's coming on.
Your first garden
and all the neighbors watch
the old house you've moved into.
If your sons toddle over to your
watering can, cigarette butts & empty
wine bottle they might think it takes
sediment, fire, wet dreams & the heads of
fish to make a garden. You're ripe

for a little work at a time: a few days
of soot & heavy moisture up from the rivers
and another night around a formica table
talking new shoots, sudden failures,
sweet furrows to nestle into and moan.

## The Bracelet

Heavy as a weapon
it wards off danger
as I walk the snowy street.
No one is going to take me by the hand.
I live in its smooth green delta.
Its black lines ring my eyes with kohl.
Its gold enters the veins of my arms.

When, like Cleopatra,
I sail out to meet him,
summer comes with me:
desire cracking the grip
of this long winter,
the heat of his hand
circling my wrist.

# On the Afternoon of the Closing
# of the Pitt Tavern

It's 3 p.m., a Wednesday,
and I'm taking my Machado & my Ritsos,
my Dickinson & Grahn
into the bathtub and I'm not getting out
till the last minute. The sun's gold
& hammered and the moon just came out
or never went in. There's snow in the air
and it's going to rain. Milliseconds at a time
we're alive despite the international military.
I'm still in love with the French—
their dark novels & tangerine drinks
slip me into a string bikini & high intellectual
conversation, even in the bathtub
and it's going to rain all night.
I'm still in love with the French
though their fashionable intellectuals
would have us pass like obedient fish
through the mind's blue waters
and I'm looking for a new tradition.
The moon hangs over Mitterand's airspace
& Reagan's ranch, guns keeping watch
from the bushes. Moon,

our statues want to reflect you,
but they're covered with weather & shit.
Where are our bronzes?
I want to deface the ugly sculpture
outside the Mellon museum
because the critics call it salvage art
but to me it looks like a maimed phallus

constructed of origami dipped in rust,
without the beauty or terror of the dead mills.
Moon, my neighbors are cutting grass
and planting bulbs. Moon, you're looking
younger; moon over the old restaurant, I'm thirsty,
but you're the driest stone I've seen.

My cousin the engineer, age 21,
leans against my stove sketching post-attack 747s
and warns me:
"Fifty percent of the country is nothing like this,"
meaning I could escape
to San Diego where the freeway
is bigger than our rivers,
or San Antonio where the mariachi bands
employ more people than USX.
Last summer in Mestre
I saw workers dump acids
into the river a mile from San Marco.
We give something up every day
for something else.
You, French, keep your airspace pure of us
while we bomb Libya,
while you train terrorists
we train replacements.

I love the dirty orange pipe
running its ribbon around J&L
because it's the one my father installed
when he was 23, first job after the War,
and the old wigshop in the Strip,
John XXIII & L. C. Greenwood on the wall.
City of pockets & cliffs,
I break my grandmother's last holy wafer
from Poland for you.
If the president wants my pity
I'll give it to him for Christmas.

If he wants this city to die
he'll never live to see it.

"Everybody likes to be stubborn,"
the urban analyst tells
two thousand ex-steel workers.
"But do you want to be crushed?"
So they move off
my comfortable street,
sell their trailers,
move South.
Patty's in South Oakland speaking into her tape recorder
all the way to the steel door.
Frank's in his cubicle worrying
he won't get there in time to eat
the last two hard-boiled eggs.
Chris cleans the barstools fifty yards from the
hospital wing where human hearts & livers wait
on dry ice for resale to mostly wealthy from countries
two days away by jet.
Chris rereads the Bill of Sale;
the students who rent from her pack up
and I knot my tie,
the one that runs down my blouse
like a sideways piano
and put on the OVA t-shirt & indigo nailpolish
and walk in there
where everybody knows me
and bury my face in Ed's wool jacket
and say "ten years."

## Hold Still

On the evening of the summer solstice
a hot breeze blows up Forbes Avenue
and the Towers Dorms jut like orange
dayglo popsicles. Suddenly a kid
strolls from around a corner
wearing something between under-
pants & a bathing suit
and he walks by us singing

SEE ME
FEEL ME
TOUCH ME
BLOW ME

He sings to the cop
lighting a cigarette
and to us. We've just heard
that once again Pittsburgh has voted
"Stairway to Heaven" the number one song
of all time, and the last radio caller
lives in Norvelt, Pennsylvania,
the town EleaNOR RooseVELT designed:

Give people an idea
Give people tools and
the country can rebuild itself.
Give each family six acres
each lot a house, coop, grape arbor.
The paper said sign up next week
and the unemployed miners came from Kecksburg,
Weltytown, became carpenters in a month.

A month ago on Pennsylvania Avenue
across from the White House
I saw an old woman washing her clothes
in a fountain. She pulled blouses & rags
from her bag, and now and then she looked up
at the great house where Capital reporters stood
on the lawn under klieg lights breathing
white balloons of moisture, waiting for the signal
to begin talking to the nation.
I saw her exhaustion and thought of Whitman
approaching the hospital tents on the long road,
marching, not wanting to enter one more tent
to take the cool cloths to the boys' faces
but he stood still and did.
You can hear the country listening for something.
Stand with friends at the office or in front of
a class or tv and watch one student stand
in front of a tank and hold off 17 tanks
behind it and imagine holding a moment
a whole country can hold

.   .   .

I touched the name of Stanislaw Drodz.
I fingered every arc & square of it.
Then I found Steve Martino.
I don't know if you're the Steve Martino
I knew—I don't know if you're the boy I knew
but I touched your name at the black wall in D.C.
in the rain while kids on tour slid by me
on the black marble sidewalk in new hightops.
The sidewalk was made for rain sliding and I'd heard
that unpredictable things happen at the wall.
People find cousins, brothers, sons
by some electromagnetic force pulling them
into the wall, though it looks, as others

have said, like a mirror no one gets inside.
I was pulled by Steve that way

when we played Guns of Navarone, Korea Vet,
any game that let us fall down onto the grass
or onto couches in our cellars on Saturdays
while our mothers did the wash. Igloos we built
during the big snows of the Fifties, like damp
cellars, were bunkers where we hoarded surplus
jackets & canteens, grenades & helmets too big
for our heads but perfect for sitting on
protecting our asses from mines & scorpions

where no bomb had ever dropped
but where the mills lay along the riversides
and even now you can hear
something that sounds like voices asking
for your voices. My grandmother would say
these are the voices of the Madonna of the Streets.
She has a face you might know, a plain face with
large bones & a crooked hairline.
She might remind you of someone you passed once
but remembered when you stood in a doorwell of your
office building leaving one world
where the touch of the city's air
moistens the eyes, and another
where the air at your table or desk
protects your secret thoughts.


The cop has carefully guided the singing boy onto a bus.
This is another lucky evening for us.
If I stand still enough I begin to think of beautiful movement
& Pavlova's explanation, in her old age,
of the urgency of learning to dance:

"One was a leaf, or a bud or a flower petal
. . . whatever the occasion demanded."